DRIP-FREE MARRIAGE DEVOTIONAL

A 31-Day Journey to a Drip-Free Covenant

DR. ELSWORTH NEALE

For permission requests, please contact:

drelsworthneale@gmail.com

This book is for educational and inspirational purposes only. It is not intended as a substitute for professional counseling, therapy, or medical advice.

Scripture quotations are taken from the King James Version (KJV), New International Version (NIV), Amplified Bible (AMP), New Living Translation (NLT), and *The Message* (MSG), unless otherwise indicated.

Published by Kingdom Lifestyle Publishers.

For more resources, visit: www.dripfreemarriage.com

DEDICATION

This book is dedicated to every couple who refuses to let love slowly leak away.

To those who are fighting for their marriage, healing from what has been broken, and choosing each other again daily.

And to the next generation, who will learn what love looks like by watching what we build today.

May your marriage not just survive, but thrive: strong, intentional, and drip-free.

TABLE OF CONTENTS

Week 3: Successful Intimacy (*Connection & Safety*)

Week 4: Covenant Strength & Legacy

INTRODUCTION

Marriage is one of God's greatest gifts and one of life's greatest responsibilities.

It begins with love, excitement, and vision. But over time, many couples discover something unexpected: it is not usually the major crises that weaken a marriage. It is the small, repeated moments that go unnoticed.

The tone that becomes sharper. The patience that grows thinner. The conversations that become shorter. The connection that slowly fades.

These are the *drips*.

Individually, they may seem insignificant. But over time, they create cracks. And if left unattended, those cracks widen into distance.

Understanding the Drip-Free Marriage System

As you walk through this devotional, you will notice that these *drips* are not random. They follow a pattern.

This pattern is called *The Drip Cycle*™.

It begins with a moment.
That moment is missed.

It leaves a mark.
That mark creates a shift.
The shift creates distance.
Distance leads to disconnection. And over time, disconnection leads to breakdown.

Most couples do not recognize the cycle until they are already deep in it.

Within that cycle, there are specific areas where breakdown tends to occur. These are known as *The 7 Marriage Leaks*™:

- *The Broken Signal*: communication without understanding
- *The Drift*: slow emotional distance
- *The Unfinished Fire*: unresolved issues beneath the surface
- *The Disrespect Shift*: loss of honor in tone and response
- *The Cold Bed*: loss of intimacy and closeness
- *The Spiritual Shift*: loss of alignment in purpose and direction
- *The Relapse Loop*: repeating patterns without lasting change

Throughout this devotional, you will begin to:

- recognize these patterns
- respond with intention
- build consistency that strengthens your relationship

This is not about perfection. It is about awareness, alignment, and daily intentionality.

This devotional was created to help you notice those drips, address them intentionally, and build a marriage that is strong, joyful, intimate, and rooted in covenant.

Over the next 31 days, you will walk through four key areas designed to help you recognize these patterns, identify the leaks, and respond with intention:

- *Awareness*: noticing what has been overlooked
- *Joy & Passion*: restoring emotional connection
- *Intimacy*: building safety and closeness
- *Covenant & Legacy*: strengthening what will last

Each day is designed to help you not only reflect, but also interrupt the cycle and build stronger patterns:

- A Scripture to anchor your heart
- A Reflection to guide your thinking
- A *Pause & Reflect* moment for personal awareness
- A Conversation Prompt to engage your spouse
- A Daily Action to apply immediately
- A Prayer to align your heart
- A Declaration to reinforce truth

This is not meant to be rushed. Take it one day at a time. Read it together if possible. Be honest in your conversations. Apply what you learn daily. Small, consistent actions will produce lasting change.

If you commit to this journey, you will not just complete a devotional. You will begin building a marriage that is intentional, resilient, and deeply connected.

A drip-free marriage is not perfect. It is consistent.

Let's begin.

WEEK 1
SPOTTING THE DRIPS

DAY 1

NOTICING THE DRIPS

Focus: The Drift and The Broken Signal

Proverbs 27:15 (KJV): *"A continual dripping on a rainy day and a contentious wife are alike."*

Reflection

Most marriages do not break suddenly. They wear down slowly.

Think about your relationship for a moment. Not the big issues, but the small ones. The tone in your voice. The way you respond when you are tired. The things you overlook instead of addressing.

These are the *drips*.

They do not seem serious at first, but over time, they shape the atmosphere of your marriage. What you ignore today quietly becomes what you live with tomorrow.

Awareness is not about blame. It is about honesty.

Pause & Reflect

What is one small behavior, yours, not your spouse's, that could be creating tension?

____

____

____

Conversation Prompt

Ask your spouse: "Is there anything small I have been doing that has been bothering you?"

Only listen. Do not explain or defend.

Today's Action

Notice one moment today when you would normally react, and choose to respond differently.

Prayer

Lord, open our eyes to the small drips in our marriage. Give us honesty without blame and courage without defensiveness. Teach us to notice what needs repair.

Declaration

We will not ignore the drips. We choose awareness as the first step toward healing.

DAY 2

SEALING THE CRACKS

Focus: The Unfinished Fire

1 Peter 4:8 (NIV): *"Above all, love each other deeply, because love covers over a multitude of sins."*

Reflection

Every marriage experiences moments of hurt. Not always big ones, sometimes just a look, a tone, or something left unsaid.

But here is the danger: what is not addressed does not disappear, it settles.

Think about the last time something hurt you. Did you address it, or carry it?

Cracks form when hurt is left unattended. But love, expressed through forgiveness and tenderness, is what seals them.

Sealing the crack does not mean pretending it did not happen. It means choosing not to let it grow.

Pause & Reflect

Is there anything small you are still holding onto?

____

____

____

Conversation Prompt

Ask your spouse: "Is there anything I have done recently that hurt you that we have not talked about?"

Listen fully. Acknowledge before responding.

Today's Action

Apologize for one thing, small or big, without explaining or defending yourself.

Prayer

Father, help us to love each other deeply. Seal our cracks with forgiveness and fill the gaps with kindness.

Declaration

Our love is the sealant. We cover one another with grace and refuse to let cracks divide us.

DAY 3

BUILDING WITH WISDOM

Focus: The Relapse Loop (early patterns)

Proverbs 24:3–4 (NLT): *"A house is built by wisdom and becomes strong through good sense. Through knowledge its rooms are filled with all sorts of precious riches and valuables."*

Reflection

A strong marriage is not built by accident. It is built intentionally.

Think about how you show up daily. Your words, your tone, your decisions.
These are your building tools.

Some days, we build with patience and understanding. Other days, we build with frustration and assumption.

The question is not whether you are building. You are.

The question is this: what are you building with?

Wisdom is choosing actions today that will create strength tomorrow.

Pause & Reflect

What have your daily actions been building in your marriage lately?

____

____

____

Conversation Prompt

Ask your spouse: "What is one thing I do that makes our relationship feel stronger?"

Receive it. Do not minimize it.

Today's Action

Do one intentional act today that strengthens your marriage, whether through encouragement, time, or support.

Prayer

Lord, give us wisdom for our home. Teach us to build with understanding, so our marriage will stand strong.

Declaration

We are intentional builders. With God's wisdom, our marriage becomes a house of strength and joy.

DAY 4

GUARDING OUR WORDS

Focus: The Broken Signal and The Disrespect Shift

Proverbs 18:21 (MSG): *"Words kill, words give life; they're either poison or fruit, you choose."*

Reflection

Think about your last few conversations with your spouse. Not what you said, but how you said it.

Tone, timing, and choice of words shape the emotional climate of your marriage more than you realize. A single careless response can linger longer than you intended. And over time, repeated words, whether harsh or kind, form patterns.

Words are not neutral. They are building something.

The question is this: what are your words producing?

Pause & Reflect

Do your words create safety or tension?

____

____

____

Conversation Prompt

Ask your spouse: "Do you feel safe with the way I speak to you?"

Do not interrupt. Do not defend. Just listen.

Today's Action

Before responding today, pause for three seconds and choose your words intentionally.

Prayer

Lord, guard our tongues. Let our words be life-giving, gentle, and wise. Help us speak in ways that build and not break.

Declaration

Our words bring life. We choose encouragement, kindness, and truth over harm.

DAY 5

QUICK TO FORGIVE

Focus: The Unfinished Fire

Colossians 3:13 (AMP): *"Bearing graciously with one another, and willingly forgiving each other… just as the Lord has forgiven you."*

Reflection

Small offenses do not always feel urgent, but they accumulate.

Think about it honestly. Are there things you have brushed off on the surface, but still feel underneath?

Unforgiveness does not always show up loudly. Sometimes it shows up as distance, silence, or reduced effort.

Forgiveness is not pretending it did not matter. It is choosing not to let it stay.

Pause & Reflect

Is there anything small or recent that you have not fully released?

____

____

____

Conversation Prompt

Ask your spouse: “Is there anything I have done that you feel I have not fully acknowledged?”

Respond with understanding, not explanation.

Today’s Action

Release one offense today through a conversation, a prayer, or a decision.

Prayer

Father, soften our hearts to forgive quickly. Help us release one another with grace and not hold onto what harms us.

Declaration

We forgive quickly. No offense will linger long enough to create distance between us.

DAY 6

THE GIFT OF PATIENCE

Focus: The Disrespect Shift

1 Corinthians 13:4 (NIV): *"Love is patient, love is kind..."*

Reflection

Patience is tested in the ordinary moments.

When your spouse is slower than you would like.
When something is not done the way you prefer.
When stress is already high.

These are the moments when impatience shows up, not because the issue is big, but because your response is unguarded.

Patience is not passive. It is a decision, a choice to slow down instead of reacting.

Pause & Reflect

When do you find yourself becoming impatient most often?

____

____

____

Conversation Prompt

Ask your spouse: "When do you feel most pressured or rushed by me?"

Listen with humility, not correction.

Today's Action

In one moment of frustration today, choose to respond calmly instead of quickly.

Prayer

Lord, clothe us with patience. Teach us to respond with calmness and grace, even when it is difficult.

Declaration

Our marriage is marked by patience. We choose calm, kindness, and grace over irritation.

DAY 7

CHOOSING PRESENCE OVER ABSENCE

Focus: The Drift

Matthew 6:21 (KJV): *"For where your treasure is, there will your heart be also."*

Reflection

You can be physically present and still be emotionally absent.

Think about your time.
Your attention.
Your focus.
What receives your best energy?

Work.
Phones.
Responsibilities.

And sometimes, unintentionally, your spouse receives what is left over.

Presence is not just being there. It is being engaged.

Pause & Reflect

When you are with your spouse, are you truly present?

____

____

____

Conversation Prompt

Ask your spouse: "Do you feel like you have my full attention when we are together?"

Receive the answer honestly.

Today's Action

Set aside at least 15 to 20 minutes today with no distractions, just focused time together.

Prayer

God, help us treasure one another through presence. Teach us to give our attention, time, and care intentionally.

Declaration

We choose presence. We give our time and attention to what matters most, each other.

WEEK 2

SPICING THE MARRIAGE (JOY & PASSION)

DAY 8

SWEETNESS OF HONEY

Focus: The Disrespect Shift

Proverbs 24:13 (AMP): *"My son, eat honey, because it is good..."*

Reflection

Think about the way you speak to your spouse on a normal day. Not when things are going well, but when you are tired, distracted, or under pressure.

Is there sweetness in your tone, or sharpness?

Sweetness in marriage is not found only in grand gestures. It is found in the small things:
A kind word.
A gentle response.
A soft tone.

These are the moments that shape how love feels each day.

Pause & Reflect

Does your presence feel pleasant or heavy?

____

____

____

Conversation Prompt

Ask your spouse: "Do my words and tone feel kind to you?"

Listen without correcting.

Today's Action

Say one intentionally kind or affirming thing today that you do not usually say.

Prayer

Lord, give us sweetness toward one another. Let our words and actions bring joy and not tension.

Declaration

Our marriage is marked by sweetness. We speak with kindness and respond with grace.

DAY 9

FRAGRANCE OF MYRRH

Focus: The Drift

Song of Solomon 1:13 (NIV): *"My beloved is to me a sachet of myrrh..."*

Reflection

Closeness is not automatic. It is cultivated.

Over time, distance can grow quietly, not through conflict, but through neglect.

Think about it: When was the last time you intentionally drew close, emotionally or physically?

Closeness requires effort. And when it is nurtured, it creates an atmosphere your spouse can feel.

Pause & Reflect

Have you been moving toward your spouse, or drifting away?

____

____

____

Conversation Prompt

Ask your spouse: “Do you feel close to me right now?”

Receive the answer honestly.

Today’s Action

Initiate one moment of closeness today through touch, conversation, or presence.

Prayer

God, make our presence comforting and desirable to one another. Restore closeness where it has faded.

Declaration

We draw close to one another. Our marriage carries the fragrance of connection and care.

DAY 10

CINNAMON & DELIGHT

Focus: The Drift

Exodus 30:23 (NLT): *"...fragrant cinnamon..."*

Reflection

Delight is often lost, not because love is gone, but because life gets heavy.

Schedules.
Responsibilities.
Stress.

And somewhere along the way, enjoyment fades.

But marriage was never meant to feel like responsibility alone. It was designed to be enjoyed.

Delight is not accidental. It is chosen.

Pause & Reflect

Do you enjoy your spouse, or do you simply coexist with them?

Conversation Prompt

Conversation Prompt

Ask your spouse: "What do we do together that you genuinely enjoy?"

Today's Action

Create one small moment of enjoyment today through laughter, a shared activity, or light conversation.

Prayer

Father, restore delight in our relationship. Help us enjoy one another again.

Declaration

We delight in each other. Joy and laughter have a place in our marriage.

DAY 11

SAFFRON & CREATIVITY

Focus: The Drift

Song of Solomon 4:14 (NIV): *"...saffron... with every kind of incense tree..."*

Reflection

Routine creates stability, but too much routine creates dullness.

Think about your relationship.
Do your days feel predictable?
Repetitive?

Creativity does not require something big. It simply requires intention.
Something new.

Something thoughtful.

Something different.

Pause & Reflect

When was the last time you did something new together?

____

____

____

Conversation Prompt

Ask your spouse: "What is one thing we could try together that would feel new or refreshing?"

Today's Action

Do one small thing differently today, something unexpected or thoughtful.

Prayer

Lord, awaken creativity in our relationship. Help us keep our love vibrant and alive.

Declaration

Our marriage is not stagnant. It is creative, fresh, and full of life.

DAY 12

FRANKINCENSE & WORSHIP

Focus: The Spiritual Shift

Matthew 2:11 (KJV): *"...gold, and frankincense, and myrrh."*

Reflection

Spiritual connection strengthens emotional connection.

When couples drift spiritually, they often drift relationally.

Think about your relationship with God, individually and together. Is He included, or only acknowledged occasionally?

Worship realigns hearts, not just toward God, but toward each other.

Pause & Reflect

Do you intentionally include God in your relationship?

____

____

____

Conversation Prompt

Ask your spouse: "How can we grow spiritually together?"

Today's Action

Pray together today, even if it is brief and simple.

Prayer

God, draw us closer to You and to each other. Let our relationship be strengthened through Your presence.

Declaration

We seek God together. Our marriage is strengthened through spiritual connection.

DAY 13

A SWEET AROMA

Focus: The Disrespect Shift and The Spiritual Shift

2 Corinthians 2:15 (AMP): *"For we are the sweet fragrance of Christ..."*

Reflection

Your marriage is not just personal. It is visible.

Others observe it.

Feel it.

Learn from it.

The way you treat each other sends a message.

Patience.

Kindness.

Respect.

These are not merely private virtues. They become a testimony.

Pause & Reflect

What does your relationship communicate to others?

____

____

____

Conversation Prompt

Ask your spouse: "What do you think others experience when they see us together?"

Today's Action

Be intentional in one public or visible interaction today through kindness, respect, or unity.

Prayer

Lord, let our marriage reflect Your love. May our relationship be a testimony of grace and unity.

Declaration

Our marriage carries the fragrance of Christ. We reflect love in how we treat each other.

DAY 14

PASSION WITHOUT SHAME

Focus: The Cold Bed and The Unfinished Fire

Hebrews 13:4 (MSG): *"Honor marriage… guard the sacredness of sexual intimacy…"*

Reflection

For many couples, intimacy is affected not only by distance, but also by discomfort, silence, or unspoken expectations.

Think about your relationship honestly. Is intimacy open and safe, or avoided and uncertain?

God designed intimacy as something good, not something hidden in shame.

But it thrives only where there is:

Trust.
Communication.
Emotional safety.

Pause & Reflect

Do you feel fully comfortable being open in this area?

____

____

____

Conversation Prompt

Ask your spouse: "Do you feel safe and comfortable talking about intimacy with me?"

Today's Action

Have one honest, respectful conversation about intimacy, without pressure or defensiveness.

Prayer

Father, remove discomfort and restore openness. Let our intimacy be safe, healthy, and honoring to You.

Declaration

We embrace intimacy without shame. Our connection is safe, open, and strengthening.

WEEK 3

SUCCESSFUL INTIMACY

(*CONNECTION & SAFETY*)

DAY 15

INTIMACY AS GOD'S DESIGN

Focus: The Cold Bed and The Drift

Genesis 2:25 (NIV): *"Adam and his wife were both naked, and they felt no shame."*

Reflection

Before sin entered the world, there was no hiding.

No fear.

No shame.

No performance.

Just openness.

Intimacy was never meant to feel pressured, confusing, or distant. It was designed to feel natural and safe.

But over time, many couples begin to hide, not physically, but emotionally.
Holding back thoughts.

Avoiding vulnerability.

Protecting themselves.

And when that happens, intimacy weakens.

Pause & Reflect

Where have you started to hold back instead of being open?

____

____

____

Conversation Prompt

Ask your spouse: "Do you feel like you can be fully open with me?"

Listen without reacting.

Today's Action

Share one honest thought or feeling you would normally keep to yourself.

Prayer

Lord, restore openness in our relationship. Help us feel safe, seen, and accepted in our vulnerability.

Declaration

We are open and unashamed. Our intimacy is built on trust and honesty.

DAY 16

LOVE WITHOUT PRESSURE

Focus: The Cold Bed

Song of Solomon 7:10 (AMP): *"I am my beloved's, and his desire is for me."*

Reflection

Desire should feel safe, not pressured.

In healthy intimacy, both partners feel wanted, not obligated.

When intimacy becomes one-sided or forced, it creates distance instead of closeness. But when it is mutual and respectful, it builds connection.

Pause & Reflect

Does intimacy feel mutual or pressured?

____

____

____

Conversation Prompt

Ask your spouse: "Do you feel desired or pressured?"

Receive this carefully.

Today's Action

Express affection today with no expectation, only care.

Prayer

God, help us create a safe and healthy space for desire. Let our connection be mutual and respectful.

Declaration

We choose mutual love. Our intimacy is safe, balanced, and honoring.

DAY 17

MUTUAL DELIGHT

Focus: The Cold Bed and The Disrespect Shift

1 Corinthians ***7:3 (NLT):*** *"The husband should fulfill his wife's needs..."*

Reflection

Intimacy is not about one person being satisfied. It is about both being valued.

When one partner feels unseen or overlooked, distance grows. But when both feel considered, delight increases.

The question is not, "Am I satisfied?"

But, "Are we both being valued?"

Pause & Reflect

Do both of you feel seen and valued in your connection?

___

___

___

Conversation Prompt

Ask your spouse: "What helps you feel valued and cared for in our relationship?"

Today's Action

Do one intentional act that prioritizes your spouse's emotional or physical needs.

Prayer

Lord, teach us to care for one another deeply. Help us create a relationship in which both feel valued.

Declaration

We honor one another. Our connection is mutual, intentional, and life-giving.

DAY 18

NO MORE SHAME

Focus: The Unfinished Fire

Romans 8:1 (NIV): *"There is now no condemnation…"*

Reflection

Many couples carry silent weight into their relationship.

Past mistakes.

Negative experiences.

Unspoken insecurities.

And even in marriage, those things can affect how they show up.

Shame does not always speak loudly, but it creates distance quietly.

God's design for marriage was never rooted in shame. It was rooted in freedom.

Pause & Reflect

Is there anything from your past affecting how you show up now?

____

____

____

____

____

____

Conversation Prompt

Ask your spouse: "Is there anything that makes it hard for you to feel fully comfortable with me?"

Respond with compassion, not correction.

Today's Action

Create a safe moment today in which your spouse feels accepted without judgment.

Prayer

Father, remove every form of shame from our relationship. Let us walk in freedom and acceptance.

Declaration

We live without condemnation. Our relationship is a safe place of acceptance and grace.

DAY 19

SACRED PLAYFULNESS

Focus: The Cold Bed and The Drift

Song of Solomon 2:16 (NIV): *"My beloved is mine, and I am his."*

Reflection

Intimacy is not only serious. It is also joyful.

Over time, many couples lose playfulness.

Everything becomes structured.

Predictable.

Routine.

But joy and lightness are part of connection.

Playfulness says, "I still enjoy you."

Pause & Reflect

Have you lost the ability to be light and playful together?

Conversation Prompt

Ask your spouse: “What makes you laugh or feel relaxed when we are together?”

Today’s Action

Create one light, playful moment today, something simple and genuine.

Prayer

Lord, restore joy and lightness in our relationship. Help us enjoy one another again.

Declaration

We choose joy. Our relationship is filled with laughter, ease, and connection.

DAY 20

PASSION AS A FIRE

Focus: The Cold Bed

Song of Solomon 8:6 (NLT): *"Love flashes like fire..."*

Reflection

Passion does not stay alive automatically.

It fades when neglected.

It strengthens when nurtured.

Many couples wait for passion to *"return,"* but passion grows through intention.

Time.

Attention.

Effort.

Pause & Reflect

Have you been expecting passion, or cultivating it?

____

____

____

Conversation Prompt

Ask your spouse: “What helps you feel most connected to me?”

Today’s Action

Create one intentional moment of connection today, planned, not accidental.

Prayer

God, reignite passion in our relationship. Teach us to nurture what we want to grow.

Declaration

Our love is alive. We nurture our connection and keep it strong.

DAY 21

BUILDING SAFETY IN LOVE

Focus: The Cold Bed and The Drift

Ephesians 5:25 (MSG): *"Husbands, go all out in your love..."*

Reflection

Intimacy cannot thrive without safety.

Safety is not only physical. It is emotional. It is knowing:

"I can be myself here."

"I will not be rejected here."

"I am respected here."

Without safety, people withdraw.

With safety, they open.

Pause & Reflect

Does your spouse feel emotionally safe with you?

____

____

____

Conversation Prompt

Ask your spouse: "Do you feel safe being fully yourself with me?"

Today's Action

Respond to your spouse today in a way that builds trust, not tension.

Prayer

Lord, help us build a relationship marked by safety and trust. Let our love reflect Your care.

Declaration

Our relationship is safe. We protect, respect, and value each other deeply.

WEEK 4

COVENANT STRENGTH & LEGACY

DAY 22

THE POWER OF TOUCH

Focus: The Cold Bed

Mark 10:16 (NIV): *"And he took the children in his arms... and blessed them."*

Reflection

Touch communicates what words sometimes cannot.

A hand held.

A hug.

A gentle tap on the shoulder.

These small moments say:

"I see you."

"I care."

"You matter."

When touch disappears, distance often grows quietly and gradually. But when touch is present, connection is reinforced daily.

Pause & Reflect

Has physical connection, especially non-sexual touch, decreased in your relationship?

Conversation Prompt

Ask your spouse: "What kind of touch makes you feel most loved?"

Today's Action

Initiate one meaningful, non-sexual touch today, whether a hug, hand-hold, or simple closeness.

Prayer

Lord, let our touch communicate love, comfort, and care. Help us stay connected in simple, meaningful ways.

Declaration

Our touch brings connection. We use it to strengthen rather than create distance.

DAY 23

DAILY OIL OF KINDNESS

Focus: The Disrespect Shift

Proverbs 31:26 (AMP): *"The teaching of kindness is on her tongue."*

Reflection

Kindness is not occasional. It is daily.

Without it, relationships become tense.

With it, they become peaceful.

Think about your tone, your responses, and your reactions.

Kindness is not weakness. It is strength under control.

Pause & Reflect

Is kindness your default response, or something you offer only occasionally?

____

____

____

Conversation Prompt

Ask your spouse: "Do you experience me as kind in everyday moments?"

Today's Action

Choose kindness in one moment when you would normally be short or impatient.

Prayer

God, make kindness our language. Let our words and actions bring peace into our home.

Declaration

Our marriage is filled with kindness. We choose gentleness over harshness.

DAY 24

STRONG COMMUNICATION

Focus: The Broken Signal

James 1:19 (NIV): *"Quick to listen, slow to speak..."*

Reflection

Communication is not just talking. It is understanding.

Many couples talk often, yet still feel unheard. Why? Because listening is often replaced with:

Preparing a response.

Defending a position.

Interrupting.

True communication happens when one person feels fully understood.

Pause & Reflect

Do you listen to understand, or to respond?

____

____

____

Conversation Prompt

Ask your spouse: “Do you feel heard when you talk to me?”

Today’s Action

In your next conversation, listen fully before responding.

Prayer

Lord, teach us to listen deeply and speak wisely. Let our communication bring us closer.

Declaration

We listen before we speak. Our communication builds understanding and connection.

DAY 25

A CORD OF THREE STRANDS

Focus: The Spiritual Shift

Ecclesiastes 4:12 (NIV): *"A cord of three strands is not quickly broken."*

Reflection

Marriage becomes stronger when it is not just two people, but three.

When God is at the center, everything changes:

Conflict is handled differently.

Decisions are made differently.

Love is expressed differently.

Without God, couples rely only on their own strength. With God, they draw from something greater.

Pause & Reflect

Is God actively included in your relationship, or only occasionally acknowledged?

____

____

____

Conversation Prompt

Ask your spouse: "How can we intentionally include God more in our relationship?"

Today's Action

Invite God into one moment today through prayer, gratitude, or a shared decision.

Prayer

Lord, be the center of our marriage. Strengthen our bond through Your presence.

Declaration

We are not alone. God is at the center of our covenant.

DAY 26

LOVE THAT ENDURES

Focus: The Spiritual Shift and The Relapse Loop

1 Corinthians 13:8 (KJV): *"Love never fails."*

Reflection

Feelings change, but love remains a choice.

There will be days when things feel easy, and days when they do not. What sustains a marriage is not emotion. It is commitment.

Enduring love says: "Even when it is hard, I am still here."

Pause & Reflect

Do you rely more on feelings, or on commitment?

____

____

____

Conversation Prompt

Ask your spouse: "What makes you feel secure in our relationship?"

Today's Action

Reassure your spouse of your commitment through words or action.

Prayer

God, strengthen our love. Help us remain committed through every season.

Declaration

Our love endures. It is steady, committed, and unshaken.

DAY 27

THE SHELTER OF COVENANT

Focus: The Drift and The Spiritual Shift

Isaiah 32:18 (NIV): *"Peaceful dwelling places... secure homes..."*

Reflection

Your marriage should feel like a safe place, not a stressful one.

A place where:

You can rest.

You can be yourself.

You can feel secure.

When tension becomes constant, home no longer feels like shelter. But covenant is designed to create safety.

Pause & Reflect

Does your relationship feel like a place of peace, or a place of pressure?

____

____

____

Conversation Prompt

Ask your spouse: "Do you feel at peace with me?"

Today's Action

Create one peaceful moment today, free from tension or conflict.

Prayer

Lord, make our home a place of peace. Let our relationship be a refuge, not a strain.

Declaration

Our marriage is a place of peace. We create safety and rest for each other.

DAY 28

PASSING ON A LEGACY

Focus: The Spiritual Shift

Psalm 145:4 (NLT): *"Let each generation tell its children…"*

Reflection

Your marriage is shaping more than your present. It is shaping the future.

Children.
Family.
Community.

They are learning from what they see.

The way you speak.

The way you forgive.

The way you love.

Pause & Reflect

What is your relationship teaching others?

Conversation Prompt

Ask your spouse: "What kind of legacy do we want our relationship to leave?"

Today's Action

Make one intentional choice today that reflects the legacy you want to build.

Prayer

God, let our marriage impact generations. Make it a reflection of Your love and faithfulness.

Declaration

We are building a legacy. Our marriage will influence others for good.

DAY 29

FRUITFUL & FLOURISHING

Focus: The Relapse Loop and The Spiritual Shift

Psalm 128:3 (NIV): *"Your wife will be like a fruitful vine..."*

Reflection

A healthy marriage produces fruit.

Not only externally, but internally:

Joy.

Peace.

Connection.

Strength.

When a relationship is nurtured, it grows. When it is neglected, it weakens.

Pause & Reflect

Is your relationship growing, or merely maintaining?

____

____

____

Conversation Prompt

Ask your spouse: “Where do you feel our relationship is growing, and where is it not?”

Today’s Action

Do one thing today that contributes to growth through connection, communication, or intentional effort.

Prayer

Lord, make our marriage fruitful. Let our relationship grow in strength, love, and unity.

Declaration

We are growing. Our marriage is alive, fruitful, and strengthening.

DAY 30

BUILT ON THE ROCK

Focus: The Spiritual Shift

Matthew 7:24 (NLT): *"Built on solid rock..."*

Reflection

Every relationship will face pressure.

Stress.

Conflict.

Unexpected challenges.

The difference is not whether storms come. It is what the relationship is built on.

If it is built on feelings, it shakes.

If it is built on truth, it stands.

Pause & Reflect

What is your relationship truly built on?

Conversation Prompt

Ask your spouse: "What do you think keeps us strong during difficult times?"

Today's Action

Reinforce one foundational habit today through prayer, communication, or connection.

Prayer

God, anchor our relationship in truth. Let nothing shake what You have built.

Declaration

We are built on a solid foundation. Our relationship will stand strong.

DAY 31

A DRIP-FREE COVENANT

Focus: All 7 Leaks (Integrated Awareness)

Colossians 3:14 (AMP): *"Love... is the perfect bond of unity."*

Reflection

A drip-free marriage is not a perfect one. It is a consistent one.

A marriage where:

Small issues are addressed.

Love is expressed daily.

Connection is intentional.

Commitment is steady.

This journey does 6not end here. It begins here.

Pause & Reflect

What will you continue doing after today?

____

____

____

Conversation Prompt

Ask your spouse: "What is one thing we want to continue as a habit moving forward?"

Today's Action

Choose one habit from this journey and commit to continuing it.

Prayer

Lord, strengthen our covenant. Help us continue building intentionally, day by day.

Declaration

We are committed. Our marriage is strong, intentional, and continually growing.

CLOSING ENCOURAGEMENT

You have completed a 31-day journey, but this is not the end.

This is where consistency begins.

Every day, you now have a choice:

Ignore the small things, or address them.

Withdraw, or connect.

React, or respond.

A strong marriage is not built in moments of intensity, but through daily intentionality. You have learned to notice the drips. You have practiced sealing the cracks. You have chosen connection, joy, intimacy, and covenant.

Now the question is not, "What did we learn?" but, "What will we continue?"

Because what you repeat becomes your pattern, and what you build consistently becomes your legacy.

Your marriage may not be perfect, but it can be intentional, growing, and unshakable. And what you build will not only impact you, it will also influence generations.

As you continue this journey, remember: this devotional is not meant to stand alone. It is part of a larger framework designed to help you understand, apply, and sustain a healthy marriage. If you are ready to go deeper, the next step is to continue building on what you have started.

Keep building.

ABOUT THE AUTHOR

Dr. Elsworth Neale is a family life educator, pastor, relationship coach, and social researcher with a passion for strengthening marriages and building healthy families.

With a unique blend of biblical insight and practical application, Dr. Neale equips couples to move beyond survival and build intentional, thriving relationships.

He is the creator of the *Drip-Free Marriage* framework, a transformational approach that helps couples identify small relational breakdowns, restore connection, and build lasting covenant strength.

Through teaching, coaching, and writing, he continues to impact individuals, couples, and communities globally.

For more resources, visit: www.dripfreemarriage.com

ADDITIONAL RESOURCES

Continue Strengthening Your Drip-Free Marriage

This devotional is designed to reinforce and apply the principles introduced in the *Drip-Free Marriage* book.

If you have not yet read the book, it is strongly recommended that you begin there in order to fully understand the framework behind this journey.

The book lays the foundation.

This devotional helps you live it.

To go deeper, explore these resources:

- *The Drip-Free Marriage Book*: the foundational teaching and framework
- *Drip-Free Marriage Journal*: a guided space for daily reflection, awareness, and intentional growth
- *Drip-Free Marriage Workbook*: practical exercises for deeper application and couple engagement
- *30-Day Drip-Free Marriage Challenge*: a guided, interactive growth experience
- *Coaching & Facilitator-Led Sessions*: personalized and group-based transformation environments

Visit: www.dripfreemarriage.com

www.ingramcontent.com/pod-product-compliance
Lightning Source LLC
LaVergne TN
LVHW011048110826
845149LV00015B/3412